Exploring Language

SERIES EDITOR: RICHARD BAIN

Cancer rate falls

Row looms over British demands

Spending squeeze

MP DEMANDS RELEASE

Exploring HEADLINES

Police enquiry into robbery

DENTISTS SAY 'NO'

It's time for some hard bargaining

GEORGE KEITH

CAMBRIDGE UNIVERSITY PRESS

Published by the Press Syndicate of the University of Cambridge
The Pitt Building, Trumpington Street, Cambridge CB2 1RP
40 West 20th Street, New York, NY 10011-4211, USA
10 Stamford Road, Oakleigh, Melbourne 3166, Australia

First published 1994

Printed in Great Britain at the University Press, Cambridge

A catalogue record for this book is available from the British Library.

ISBN 0 521 44623 6 paperback

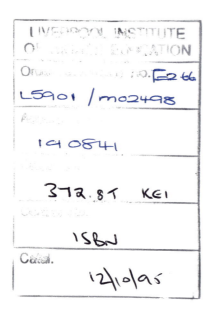
Acknowledgements

Thanks are due to the following for permission to reproduce copyright materials:

The British Library; *Daily Mirror*; *The Times*; *Today Newspaper*; the *Independent*; Minolta (UK) Ltd.

Every effort has been made to reach copyright holders. The publishers would be glad to hear from anyone whose rights they may have unknowingly infringed.

Contents

Exploring headlines

The first part of this book provides texts and headlines drawn from a variety of newspapers.

In the second part of the book you will find activities that require you to explore the texts and the headlines in some detail.

Often you will be asked to collect and explore examples you have found yourself. The examples in this book are only starting points for finding out and for testing your own ideas: the really important examples are the ones you discover for yourself.

Remember that there are many newspapers in print: daily and weekly; local and national. Make sure you explore a wide range, not just one or two of the same kind.

Try finding out just how many national papers are published each day in Britain. You could guess to begin with, although a newsagent would be able to tell you more accurately. Aim to get one example of each to form a reference library.

You could also find out what daily, weekly and half-weekly papers are published in your area. Look out, too, for papers that are delivered free.

Your explorations using this book will be all the more interesting and worthwhile if they are thorough. Make a note of the date of publication and the newspaper it came from on the back of each article you collect.

Saddam's big guns blown up

By MARK DOWDNEY

SADDAM Hussein's superguns were destroyed yesterday under the supervision of United Nations inspectors.

The giant weapons - parts of them made in Britain - were cut to pieces and blown up.

The biggest, not yet assembled, would have been capable of blasting huge shells into Israel, Saudi Arabia and Iran.

Its components were found south of Baghdad.

A gun with a 165ft barrel, discovered at a well-camouflaged mountain site to the north, had been test-fired by the Iraqis.

Its missiles covered 160 miles.

The superguns were destroyed under ceasefire terms agreed by Saddam at the end of the Gulf War.

Inspectors have also located dozens of Scud launcher sites also earmarked for destruction.

Phoney book

PHONE chiefs have halted distribution of 128,000 new directories in Reading, Berks, because of a wrong number.

SILLY SUD! SOAP STAR ENDS UP 300 MILES ADRIFT

AUSSIE soap star Alan Dale felt a right wallaby when he set off for Stonehenge – and missed it by 300 miles.

He gave up after his thirst for English history turned into a geography lesson with all the twists and turns of a Neighbours storyline.

Touring actor Alan - Ramsay Street's Jim Robinson - pulled into town convinced he was almost at the ancient **WILTSHIRE** site.

Bemused bobbies in Richmond, **NORTH YORKSHIRE**, told him that he was in fact nearer to Emmerdale.

A police spokesman said "We tried to put him right about driving in Britain and advised him to break the journey."

Mistake

Shrugging off his mistake Alan, 44, told them: "No problem. I'm used to driving long distances in Australia."

But within a few miles he drove straight into another time-honoured feature of English life – roadworks on the A1.

Alan's quest for Stonehenge started from Kirkcaldy, **FIFE**, where he finished a three-week

MIXED-UP: Alan

By CLIVE CRICKMER

tour with the comedy play Caravan.

He finally gave up at Stratford-on-Avon in **WARWICKSHIRE** and phoned his British agent Joan Brown.

Joan said: "He wanted to do some sight-seeing and I suggested the Lake District and Yorkshire Dales.

"But where Stonehenge comes in, I just don't know. He seems to have got rather confused."

A Richmond police spokesman said: "A lot of tourists drop in to ask directions, though they don't often get this lost."

NOT FARE, BR

TRAIN fare increases of up to seven per cent sought by British Rail boss Sir Bob Reid from January should be halved, passenger watchdog leaders demanded yesterday.

BOSS: Reid

RAIN RAP FOR SPAIN

TOURIST chiefs in Spain got a roasting yesterday for promising holidaymakers eternal sunshine.

The Advertising Standards Authority upheld a complaint over a magazine advert praising the "unrivalled peace of northern Spain."

It added: "But one thing never changes. The ever present sun." A woman

reader told the advertising watchdog the region had at least 11 days of rain each month.

German Porras, of the Spanish Tourist Office, said: "It was probably just someone taking a bit of poetic licence."

Easy come, easy go . . easy rider

By JO BECKERLEY

ROYAL biker Lord Linley isn't one to let a little thing like the theft of his £10,000 Harley Davidson get him down.

He just strolled down to a Park Lane dealers, picked up this £7,500 **BMW** - on approval, naturally - and was back on the road in under a week.

Of course, Princess Margaret's speed-loving son wasn't exactly stuck for transport. He has an Aston Martin, a Range Rover and a soft-top Morris Minor at home to choose from.

But when it comes to catching the ladies' eyes, the 29-year-old viscount has discovered that a two-wheeled mean machine leaves no vroom for improvement. The leather-clad Lord had only just picked up the bike when he arrived at his London furniture shop yesterday.

But judging by the spare helmet tucked under his arm, the royal bachelor had already settled on a pillion partner.

Picture JASON FRASER

DI'S SOLE MATE

By JAMES WHITAKER

A MAN stepped forward yesterday to tell Princess Diana he makes her shoes.

"I recognise what you are wearing," said Don Parker. "How are they?"

"Very comfortable," Di replied. "But, don't forget, I always have to have a small heel because of my height."

Don, 58, works for the Queen's shoemakers Rayne and cuts leather for Diana's size 7 shoes. His efforts won royal approval during the princess's visit to a Barnardo's project in London.

PLEASED: Diana

★ ★ ★ ★

Bodybuilding champ killed by heart attack

A BODYBUILDER collapsed and died from a heart attack as he warmed up for a Mr England contest.

Andy Hornby, who was tipped to take the title, slumped to the ground 30 minutes before he was due on stage. The 23-year-old former junior Mr Universe's death was thought to be caused

by ANDREW RUSSELL

by an imbalance of salts in his body caused by crash-dieting.

Mr Hornby's fiancee Theresa Thornton, 23, who lived with him in Wallsend, near Newcastle upon Tyne, was in the audience at the Gateshead Leisure Centre. She travelled with him in the ambulance to hospital,

but he was dead on arrival. They had planned to marry next year.

Mr Hornby, who was 6ft 1in tall and weighed 16 stone, had hoped the championship would be a step towards his dream of becoming Mr Universe.

The self-employed milkman took up bodybuilding as an eight-stone 14-year-old at Newcastle's Gold Star gym.

Yesterday gym owner Rafik Caprelian said: "When I saw him before the contest he was in superb condition.

"I have no doubt he would have gone on to win the Mr Universe title."

Mr Caprelian said a rapid loss of weight in the 12 weeks before the contest could have triggered Mr Hornby's death.

"It is not uncommon for bodybuilders to lose about three stones to improve their muscle definition," he said.

Dangerous

"The only way to reduce the fat levels and water content of your body is by strict dieting and exercise.

"But if you are not careful you can put a tremendous strain on the body, and sometimes the heart can't take that pressure."

In a similar incident four years ago Mr Hornby became dehydrated during a flight to America for the Junior Mr World competition.

The potassium in his body rose to a dangerous level and he had to be rushed to hospital.

"Andy was absolutely dedicated to the sport," said Mr Caprelian.

"He would never have touched steroids. It is a great tragedy."

TITLE DREAM: Tragic bodybuilder Andy Hornby

Storms wipe out seal pups

HUNDREDS of baby seals have been wiped out by storms which battered the beaches where they were born.

White pups have been found dead, dying or abandoned on the Shetlands. The area's 3,500 grey seals normally produce about 500 pups a season but it is feared more than half have died.

Only the "amazing" response from islanders had prevented an even greater tragedy, said the Nature Conservancy Council.

Jan Morgan, who runs a sanctuary on the mainland village of Hillswick, said she normally cared for about six orphans but had received over 30 in the past fortnight.

Gales lashed breeding grounds at the peak of the pupping season, said scientist Eileen Stuart. The islands' seal population is still recovering from a virus three years ago which greatly reduced numbers.

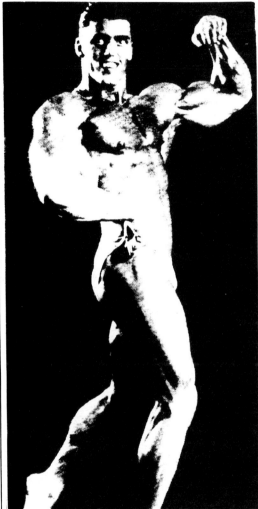

TRAGIC CHAMP: Contest favourite Andy died minutes before going on stage

'Heart attack' tragedy as Andy, 23, limbers up

By MIRROR REPORTER

TOP muscleman Andy Hornby collapsed and died minutes before he was due to compete in the Mr England bodybuilding contest.

Sixteen-stone Andy, 23, died in his girlfriend's arms after being taken ill as he limbered up in a corridor. It is thought he suffered a massive heart attack.

The ex-junior Mr Universe had been tipped to win the Mr England title ahead of 70 other competitors. But he collapsed as girlfriend Theresa Thornton helped him outside for some air and died as he was rushed to hospital.

The tragedy stunned an audience of 1,500 at the Gateshead Leisure Centre, Tyne and Wear, on Saturday.

Organiser Karl Willams said: "Andy was very popular and we decided to go on with the show in his memory.

"But everyone was very subdued. Everyone who knew him felt his death deeply."

Last night Theresa was too distraught to talk at the home she shared with Andy in Wallsend, Tyne and Wear.

But his father, Ken, 50, dismissed suggestions that Andy, a milkman, may have been using body-building drugs.

He said: "He lived for the sport and had been training hard for this contest for six months.

"There is no way he would have jeopardised all that."

Devastated

Andy's mother June added: "At least he died doing what he loved. We are absolutely devastated. He was such a fit young man."

Andy's coach Rafik Caprelia said rapid weight loss in the 12 weeks before the contest could have triggered his death.

He said: "It is not uncommon for body-builders to need to lose about three stones to improve their muscle definition.

"If you are not careful you can put a tremendous strain on the body and sometimes the heart can't take the pressure."

Four years ago Andy was rushed to hospital after dehydrating as he flew to America for the Junior Mr World Contest.

An inquest is expected to be opened today.

ZANY Michael Jackson got such a kick out of Liz Taylor's wedding that he is now arranging one of his own.

But his will be a mock ceremony – with Jacko as the groom and movie star Brooke Shields as the bride.

The way-out pop star gave Liz away when she married Larry Fortensky at Jacko's Californian estate on October 7.

GROOM: Jacko

The next day, still elated, Jacko "proposed" to old flame Brooke, according to the National Enquirer.

Startled Brooke, 26, said she didn't want to get married – but Jacko, 33, told her it would not be a real wedding.

And she could always say: "I don't."

Giggling Brooke agreed to be the bride – probably at Christmas.

By CHRISTIAN GYSIN

MILLIONAIRE soccer star Peter Shilton talked last night about his mortgage difficulties.

It was alleged that he was behind with payments on his luxury home.

But Shilton, 42, said: "There was a misunderstanding over some payments which should have been made.

"I received a letter telling me there could be a court appearance over the missed payments.

"This was an administrative error nothing more. I have paid the money owed and everything has been sorted out."

The former England goalkeeper, who earns around £250,000 a year with Second Division

LETTER: Shilton

Derby County, is a keen horse racing fan and enjoys gambling and the good life.

A Derby County insider said last night: "Peter lives life to the full he earns big, but he spends as big."

Asked about his love of horses and gambling, Shilton said: "How I spend my money is my business.

"I've no comment about that."

The mortgage payments related to his home in Loughborough, Leics, nicknamed Shilton Towers and described as palatial by fellow footballers.

Shilton owns three other properties in Leicester, Southampton and Hampshire.

D

FOREIGN Secretary Douglas Hurd indicated last night that a November election is on the cards.

He said the tide has turned against Labour and is moving towards the Government.

"I detect a clear tide of opinion which believes that it is John Major who offers the right leadership for our country," Mr Hurd told Tories in Witney, Oxfordshire.

It is the lift in the economy and failure of Labour which is changing people's views, he added. "Labour offers the choice of a leader without a credible party, or a party without a credible leader."

The Poll debate: Page 6

RUSSIAN president Boris Yeltsin was last night said to be suffering from a "minor heart problem" after being taken ill in his office.

His secretary denied earlier reports he had been taken to hospital from the parliament building, but admitted he had to take the day off work.

He said: "He has a minor heart problem and went home to rest.

The secretary said that Mr Yeltsin would be going ahead with a planned address to the Russian Federation's parliament today. Sources said other items on his agenda would remain unchanged.

MAJOR structural defects aboard Britain's nuclear-powered Polaris submarines have been hidden from MPs, a former atomic safety chief claims.

The fleet is crippled by reactor leaks, and affected vessels are banned from foreign ports without special permission.

At least two of the submarines have been refused safety certificates and the others only have a temporary licence, claims Reginald Farmer, former UK Atomic Authority safety chief, on ITV's This Week tonight.

A BANK customer who claimed money from his account disappeared through a cash dispenser was awarded compensation yesterday in the first case of its kind.

Outdoor instructor John Allan, 28, sued the Bank of Scotland after £570 vanished from his account.

The missing cash had been withdrawn in eight transactions from an electronic 'hole-in-the-wall' machine.

Three of the pay-outs hap-

by IAN FLETCHER
Consumer Correspondent

pened when Mr Allan was out of the country on a skiing trip.

"I knew I had not made these withdrawals," said Mr Allan, of Cleland, Strathclyde.

"They just maintain their machines don't make mistakes."

He opted for legal action after the bank refused to compensate him and the Banking Ombudsman also rejected his case. An out-of-court settle-

ment was reached after the Consumers' Association backed his claim.

They had planned to call evidence from a computer expert who would, it was claimed, show the cash machines could go wrong.

CA legal services director David Tench said: "The terms are confidential but Mr Allan is a very happy man.

"These machines are very, very rarely fallible but this puts the financial institutions in a very considerable dilemma. Maybe we will have to

queue up again for our money at the counter and none of us will like that."

● Credit card holders will soon be writing out a cheque instead of flashing their plastic in stores.

Barclaycard are to introduce distinctive cheque books for eight million customers throughout the UK.

This will mean that people can use the cheques in places which don't accept credit cards.

A spokesman said: "This will help fill the gap."

FIFTY-SEVEN families were last night preparing to abandon their homes within 24 hours after deadly asbestos was discovered on a council estate.

They were advised to have immediate medical checks but a leading chest expert warned they face a health "timebomb" which could explode in 20 or 30 years time.

Dangerously high levels of asbestos, including the most dangerous, blue asbestos, which causes lung disease and lung cancer, were discovered in air and soil samples taken from the Lumdsen Road estate in Portsmouth, Hampshire.

It was just five years ago when the Department of the Environment gave the are the all-clear. But last night Government experts warned that anyone who comes into contact with the soil — especially young children — could be at risk.

The houses had been built on a former rubbish dump where asbestos waste was once buried. Local environmental heath officer Alan Higgins said: "A covering was laid over the materials but the report

by CLIVE NELSON
and NICKI POPE

has shown this to be inadequate in some areas or not present at all."

The families, including the wives and children of 12 Royal Navy ratings, will be moved into temporary accommodation.

Council housing chairman, Brian Pope, said: "It is a precautionary measure to safeguard them. We wanted to act as quickly as possible."

Residents claimed last night that they had been "kept in the dark" by council officials.

Mother-of-five Pat Taylor, 35, said: "We knew they were carrying out tests but we were not told what they were for. Now, we are told to get out within 24 hours."

She added: "There has always been a lot of sickness and diarrhoea around here among the children but we have put it down to being near the sea — now we may have the real reason.

"No-one ever said there was any danger. I feel we were just dumped down

here to get us out of the way. Some of the naval homes have been boarded up but we are still here."

Neighbour Paula Scotney, 32, added: "I have seen council houses empty around this city, but they have left us down here.

"Our children have been playing around here and now they tell us that it is not safe and that we should go an see out doctors.

"Why wasn't something done before? This has turned our lives upside down."

Portsmouth is one of the nation's "hotspots" for asbestos disease, chest expert Dr Sherwood Budge said last night. But it is also on the increase in many other ports, including Plymouth, Liverpool, Southampton and Chatham, Kent, where asbestos was used to insulate ships and prevent burning.

Dr Budge said the risk of disease was slight, but added: "There is no point in sending people to their GP now because it is highly unlikely that anybody will have anything detectable.

"If they have been exposed for the last five years, it will be 20 or 30 years before the disease will become evident."

From Page 1

Saddam is resisting. There is concern he believes the West has lost interest in Iraq because of the break-up of the Soviet Union and the Yugoslav crisis.

Talks are still underway with Iraq's representative to the UN in the hope of reaching agreement over warfare site inspections and averting new hostilities.

A US official said: "The resolution makes quite clear that the UN can use its own helicopters and therefore the Iraqs are not in a position to say no."

White House spokesman Marlin Fitzwater said President Bush had conferred with Saudi Arabia's King

Fahd over sending jets back to the Saudi desert.

"I don't think it's an offensive kind of operation. I'm not sure there's a decision to do anything, just to be in place," he added."

While the Allies want a peaceful solution, sources stressed that contingency plans were drawn up and could be "dusted off" at any stage. There are still 33,000 US troops in the Gulf region, 5,000 of them in the air force.

General John Galvin, Supreme Allied Commander in Europe, confirmed in an interview on NBC television renewed military action in the Gulf was "possible".

"It all depends on Saddam," he said.

ANGRY shareholders lashed out at an electricity company's chief yesterday when he refused to disclose his salary.

Norweb chairman Ken Harvey defended directors' pay at the annual meeting in Manchester.

He said: "They are salaries which are essential if we are to retain our directors."

The annual report showed 50-year-old Mr Harvey's salary went up to £105,135 last year – a rise believed to be around 60 per cent.

WEATHER 26 ● TELEVISION 28 & 29 ● NEWSDESK

E

HEART WIDOW'S £350,000 PAY-OUT

Wartime airman's Dresden shame and rage

Farm pesticides safety plan reaps toxic harvest

Everest rubbish problem peaks

Builders' jobs gloom deepens

Compact disc deals squeeze small traders

Revenge clue to shooting of postman

Dramatic surge in assault figures

VIOLENCE SHOCK

Street battleaxe Ivy is set to quit

STRANDED BRITS FLEE RIOT TERROR

Staple-gun surgeon in cancer op revolution

RAIL BRIDGE PLUNGE HORROR

Afghan election deal rejected

NEW TOP PAY RISE SCANDAL

Women track athletes gaining ground on men

MOTORBIKE MADNESS TAKES TO THE HIGH SEAS

GIRL, 16, IN GIFT MOTOR HORROR

Court drama of granny in heart appeal swindle case

Immigrant aid group to discuss 'dilemma' offer

Software piracy police mean business

Dead tot sister's agony

THE INDEPENDENT

Fi

★★★★ Published in London   40p

No 1,755

TUESDAY 2 JUNE 1992

SUMMARY

HOME

Tender services: William Waldegrave said that the Government wanted to extend competitive tendering from local authorities' "blue-collar" services to the white-collar professions, as reported in this week's *Independent on Sunday* — Page 6

Legal fraud: Solicitors may have to pay a special levy to meet rising claims against dishonest lawyers — Page 2

Religious leisure: Britain's most exclusive country club has 500 members ... all clergy — Page 8

FOREIGN

Ring of fire: A Serbian general says Belgrade is "ringed with rockets", ready to repulse any Western military intervention — Page 10

Beregovoy survives: The Socialist government in France survived a vote of censure, despite Communist support for the opposition, by three votes — Page 10

'Not Ivan': John Demjanjuk presented new evidence in a Jerusalem court to prove he was not the Nazi war criminal Ivan the Terrible — Page 10

BUSINESS

VAT discord: The Treasury and the European Commission appear at loggerheads over an EC proposal to harmonise VAT rates — Page 20

SPORT

Sweeping clean: The England manager Graham Taylor has named his side to meet Finland tomorrow and says it is the one he will field in the opening European Championship match against Denmark. In come John Barnes and Gary Stevens, and the sweeper system — Page 30

TRANSPORT

Getting where? Sir Alfred Sherman believes that a subsidised, nominally

---

'Dustbin' jail should be modernised or closed down, Chief Inspector of Prisons says

Clarke rejects call for reform at Dartmoor

Dartmoor: 'No prison has had a more melancholy history ... It offers prisoners very little and demands conformity at the risk of severe penalties'   *Photograph: Tom Pilston*

By Nick Cohen
Home Affairs Reporter

DARTMOOR PRISON is a penal "dustbin" which should be shut by the end of next year if it has not been radically transformed into a community jail, according to Judge Stephen Tumim, the Chief Inspector of Prisons.

Community prisons, which take only local prisoners, were proposed by Lord Justice Woolf's report after the 1990 riots at Strangeways, Dartmoor and other English jails. The aim is to encourage responsible behaviour and

Food was left in open containers on the kitchen floor near waste and cockroaches. The risk of dis-

"The austere building, the wildness of the country and above all its reputation as the end of the road for trouble-making prisoners" have contributed to a macho culture "which offers prisoners very little and demands confor-

---

PM rules out devolution for Scotland

By Anthony Bevins
Political Editor

JOHN MAJOR urged the Scottish people to step back from demands for devolution yesterday. He gave his most powerful warning yet that while a United Kingdom could continue to work "at the hinge of history", nationalist fragmentation would plunge in an unknown and inglorious future.

The Prime Minister told a meeting of the Ayrshire Chamber of Commerce at Prestwick that as long as Scotland and England, Wales and Northern Ireland stood together, they could build democracy and promote the principles of democracy and freedom in an uncertain world.

Narrow-minded nationalism, on the other hand, "would weaken all the countries of this kingdom. It would send them sliding, diminished and divided, down separate paths towards an unknown and inglorious future."

Echoing the advice that he had given against a Czech-Slovak split in Prague last week, Mr Major said separation would relegate Scotland to the outer fringe of the European Community. Scotland alone could not have "packed the same punch" in EC negotiations. The Prime Minister said: "The lesson is clear: because we have stood together in Europe, we have gained together."

But Mr Major also warned that separation would tragically sideline Britain, too. "at the very time when the world is struggling to build a new order."

With the UK taking on the presidency of the EC from July, he would be preparing the way for an enlargement that could see Poland, Czechoslovakia and Hungary taking on full EC membership within the next decade.

"I also want to begin to roll back unnecessary regulation by Brussels that is placing too many burdens on business . . . We have long fought interfering regulation at home; it is now time to take our campaign into Europe."

Britain's pivotal role in the EC, with more influence than ever before, would be jeopardised by sep-

half-way step across a chasm. Anyone minded to take that step should look over the edge at the consequences into which we might all be plunged. They would see the is safety net".

He said: "You could not bolt on a second parliament to our constitution without altering its whole delicate balance. The future status and number of Scotland's MPs at Westminster would inevitably be affected. The present distribution of the United Kingdom's finance would inevitably be affected. It would be a dangerous and divisive road for us all."

Yet he said that Labour was "splitting apart" in Scotland, and while some members of the Opposition remained cautious, others were lining up with the nationalist left to push Scotland down the road to isolation.

The Prime Minister then emphasised the great degree of devolution already enjoyed by Scotland. "Her own legal system. Her own education system. Scottish banks. Scottish churches. Her own Home Department. her own institutions in the UK Parliament; her own system of local government, too. Scotland is a nation; and she does not need to turn to separatism to prove it."

But he also underlined his own pre-election commitment to a continuing process of stocktaking-listening to all the voices in Scotland — "not just the loudest".

Mr Major said his passionate commitment to a defence of the Union did not preclude evolutionary change in government.

And he appeared to concede that the perception of London's remoteness from Scotland was something that had to be tackled. While Scottish interests were always "strongly in our minds" he wanted that to be seen and felt.

"Already in this parliament," Mr Major said, "we have begun to bring more openness to the conduct of Whitehall. I want govern-

privatised British Rail could produce the worst of all worlds – *Page 19*

SCIENCE AWARD

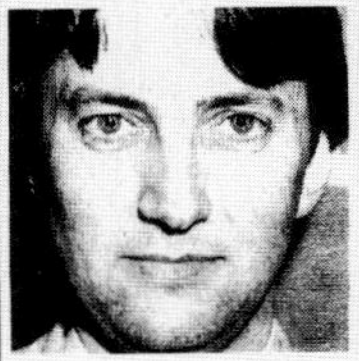

Second accolade: Tom Wilkie, the Science Editor of *The Independent*, yesterday received the Science Writers Award from Glaxo and the Association of British Science Writers, for his profile of Michael Faraday. It is the second time he has been a prizewinner – *Page 2*

LIVING

In her own write: "For a long time I was devastated. I believed he'd earned and deserved the right to be Prime Minister, and that he would have made a very good one." *Hunter Davies talks to Glenys Kinnock, and finds her ready to write a book – Page 14*

TOMORROW

Mid-life crisis: "I'm quite sure that the benefits of HRT to me have been at the expense of my husband. I'm just as keen on sex now as I was in my twenties, and he just isn't as potent any more." *Ruth Hughes finds women enjoying a new lease of life after hormone replacement therapy, but at what cost?*

CONTENTS

23
9 770951 946023

But the call for fundamental reform from the widely respected watchdog, published today, has already been flatly rejected by Kenneth Clarke, the Home Secretary. Mr Clarke dismisses changing the prison's status as impractical, and adds that nevertheless there is no question of closing the 183-year-old jail.

In an inspectorate report on Dartmoor, Judge Tumim says the jail cannot carry on being a dumping-ground for prisoners from as far away as Yorkshire. Its "only possible long-term future" is as a community prison for the West Country with specialised units for vulnerable inmates. "If such a prison is not wanted then Dartmoor should be closed," Judge Tumim says.

emotional stability by keeping inmates where they can maintain close links with their families.

However, Mr Clark replies: "[Dartmoor] is too big to become a community prison in the way the Chief Inspector recommends. There are too few centres of population in the South-west to fill it." He also rejects a further recommendation that the prison's security status should be downgraded, although he does add that work to develop specialised units is under way.

The judge is understood to have been so appalled by conditions in Dartmoor that he was close to recommending its immediate closure. He found prisoners scrubbing dishes with the same brushes they used to clean lavatories.

ease was high. He decided the jail should be given a last chance, but his report makes it clear that Dartmoor, opened in 1809 to house French prisoners of war, will find it exceptionally difficult to improve its standards.

"No prison has had a more melancholy or chequered history, nor is located more remotely from the homes of the prisoners it presently holds," he says. Change will require leadership of the highest calibre.

But although there are a few "amazingly resilient managers", most senior staff show "understandable signs of being worn out by the traditional culture" of a jail that has been turned into a dustbin for "prisoners no other institution wants to take.

mity at the risk of severe penalties. In these circumstances confrontation between staff and inmates is often the only satisfaction."

Mr Clarke has rejected the report because the Home Office was committed to spending £25m on refurbishing Dartmoor before the Woolf inquiry finished its work and issued its call for community prisons. Judge Tumim says that the spending will "be wasted unless it is matched by a commitment to create a positive and purposeful regime. [Dartmoor] has a long way to go very fast if it is to be shown that the money was sensibly invested."

The programme to fit lavatories in all cells was two years behind schedule at the time of the inspection. The Home Office says it is

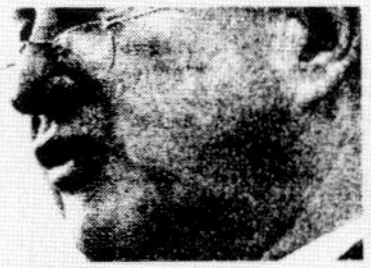

Judge Tumim: 'End of the road for trouble-making prisoners'

now back on target. Mr Clarke says Dartmoor's notoriety still colours public perceptions of the prison, obscuring some of the "good work" being done there. The refurbishment programme is raising standards of hygiene and will remove the faults in the washroom and kitchen Judge Tumim identifies.

aratism at home. But Mr Major went further, arguing that Britain's special authority in the UN would also end, her Commonwealth influence would be weakened, and her contribution to world debates on the environment, trade and debt would be stifled. As for devolution, Mr Major said that was a half-way step – "a

ment in the 1990s to be accessible and responsive to the people throughout our country.

"And where improvements can be made – in Scotland, England, Northern Ireland or Wales – we will make them. But with me you can be sure of this: I will not weaken Scotland. And that means I will not weaken the Union."

Taylor tells of Ward case offer

LORD TAYLOR, the Lord Chief Justice, yesterday revealed that he had been willing to give evidence at Judith Ward's appeal hearing, but this unprecedented offer by the country's most senior judge was turned down by the Director of Public Prosecutions, Barbara Mills QC. In an interview with *The Independent*, Lord Taylor went on to support calls for changes to restore confidence in the criminal justice system, including independent supervision of the police, an end to uncorroborated confessions, improved access to forensic science, and changes to the role of the Court of Appeal.

Interview, page 6

Bush pledges aid to save forests

By David Usborne
in Washington
and Nicholas Schoon
in London

PRESIDENT George Bush, seeking to deflect criticism of US indifference towards the Earth Summit beginning tomorrow in Rio, yesterday called for international spending on forest protection to be doubled.

Mr Bush pledged that the US would make a "down-payment" of an additional $150m (£80m) next year on top of the $120m already earmarked in the 1993 US budget for aid to countries with threatened forests, and would seek to persuade other developed nations to make similar commitments. "At Rio, I will ask other industrialised countries to join me in doubling world-wide forest assistance with the goal of halting the loss of the world's forests by the end of the decade," Mr Bush said.

The initiative has clearly been devised to forestall criticism of Mr Bush's environmental record when he visits the summit at the end of next week. It also helps the President to tread the domestic political tightrope between voters' demands for economic recovery and action on the environment.

An indication that the Bush administration may already have strayed too far from voters came in a *USA Today* poll yesterday, which suggested that 58 per cent of Americans would have supported a far-reaching treaty on global warming, even if it meant denting the US economy.

Mr Bush has come under fierce attack from environmentalists, first for dithering over whether to attend the Rio summit, and then for persuading other countries to water down a planned declaration on global warming. Last Friday, the US administration said it would not support another text on maintaining the world diversity of species of animals and plants.

That sparked a world-wide dispute over whether leading developed nations would sign a treaty

TOMORROW and for the next 12 days *Independent* writers will give comprehensive daily coverage of the Earth Summit from Rio.

in Rio aimed at protecting the Earth's fauna and flora. Yesterday John Major added his voice to the chorus of sceptics, warning that some people were expecting too much of the Earth Summit.

But White House officials insisted that Mr Bush's latest initiative would provide a great boost to the environment. "This will amount to a significant investment

over the next decade, putting us on the path toward our ultimate goal of halting the loss of the world's forests," one said. If other donor nations take up the challenge, international commitments could increase from $1.35bn to $2.7bn annually.

The administration experts also suggested that in helping to save the world's forests, estimated to be vanishing at the rate of 79 acres a minute, the international community would automatically fulfill many of the aims of both the global warming and biodiversity treaties.

Mr Bush, who made the announcement during a speech at the Goddard Space Centre in Maryland, added that he would call for an international "Forest Partnership Forum" later this year to discuss joint action.

Further reports, page 12
Leading article, letters, page 18

Labour warned on union cash

By Barrie Clement
Labour Editor

UNIONS will stop funding Labour if their voting power within the party is abolished, according to the key link-man between the two wings of the movement.

Tom Sawyer, deputy general secretary of the public service union Nupe and a senior adviser to Neil Kinnock, yesterday delivered a blunt warning to Labour leadership candidates: "No say, no pay." Mr Sawyer, who chairs Labour's influential home policy committee, added: "While we fund the party, we'll have a say – it's as crude as that."

The Conservatives are likely to seize on Mr Sawyer's bluntness as evidence that the party remains in hock to its traditional paymasters.

In a speech to his union's annual conference in Scarborough, he attacked union leaders backing radical reform of the relationship between party and unions. With a touch of what he described as "northern sophistication", he said: "If you've got nothing to say to help the party, shut your gob."

Mr Sawyer was thought to be addressing in particular John Edmonds, leader of the GMB general union, and Bill Jordan, president of the Amalgamated Engineering and Electrical Union, who has urged abolition of the union block vote, which commands 40 per cent of the electoral college for party leaders and 90 per cent of the policy-making vote.

Mr Sawyer, who has borne much of the burden of ensuring the Kinnock reforms of party policy won union backing over the past four years, endorsed the intended reduction of the block vote at annual conferences from 90 to 70 per cent. But he saw no immediate reason for further reduction, at least without thorough debate.

In contradiction to John Smith, the leading contender for the Labour leadership, Mr Sawyer endorsed the electoral college system. He added, however, that it should be democratised. Both individual party members and trade unionists who paid the political levy should participate in the democratic process.

Mr Sawyer rounded on those who blamed the unions for Labour's election defeat. "If the campaign wasn't good enough, it was the politicians who were in charge of the campaign that failed. That's the real truth."

Later Mr Sawyer told journalists that there was a case for modernising the link between the two wings of the movement, "and not casting block votes on behalf of anonymous people". But he was not prepared to enter an auction with other union leaders "bidding the block vote down".

Everlasting light bulb cuts out glowing pains

From Phil Reeves in Los Angeles

AN END could be near to the maddening business of stumbling around in the dark looking for a candle because the light has inexplicably blown during a dinner party. A new type of household light bulb is being pioneered which its inventors claim will last for 14 years.

Its developers say that it glows as brightly as the traditional light bulb, switches on and off instantly, fits into ordinary sockets and can even be dimmed seductively. The light bulb is also said to use about a quarter of the electricity that powers the orthodox "incandescent" household bulb and could dramatically reduce energy consumption and pollution caused by power stations.

The "E-lamp" has been developed by Intersource Technologies, of Sunnyvale, California, backed by American Electric Power Co of Columbus, Ohio, which plans to manufacture it by the million. Intersource's spokesman described it as the biggest technological breakthrough in lighting since Thomas Edison managed to make a filament glow without interruption in 1879.

Unlike the ordinary bulb, the E-Lamp has no filament – the main cause of bulb failure – but operates using a high-frequency radio signal. This is generated by a magnetic coil, and passed through a gas converting it into a plasma. The energy emitted strikes a phosphorus coating on the glass, causing it to glow merrily.

Work on the technology has been going on for some years but until now no one has found a way of using radio waves without interfering with other devices near by such as television sets and stereos.

The E-lamp's lifespan is estimated at 20,000 hours – 14 years of average use, and 20 times the life of the standard light bulb. It is expected to cost between $10 (£6) and $20 when it goes on the market next year.

Kohl set for further battle over strike threat by engineers

Militant sets its sights on union post

BAA set to double Heathrow's scope

Civil servants set for Docklands

Baghdad military poised to thwart Kurdish elections

Cars arson set to boost insurance premiums

CARLING'S MEN OF COURAGE

GOOD BOYOS

All together now..
OUR KEN'S NOT BORING

The filth they left behind could cost thousands to clear
DISGUSTING

Britain snubs EC declaration

Electricity price rises denounced as 'racket'

"It's Kylie......... Bidding to be the new Madonna" You ain't got the material girl!

YOU
Bread star is branded
COWARD

BIG BROTHER'S BLACKLIST
22,000 names are on top secret 'Don't employ' file

Maxwell on fiddle at *DAILY NEWS*

DON'T RIP HEART OUT OF BRITAIN

HEARTLESS
Queen's disabled workers thrown on the scrapheap

Reward offered for missing ponies
HEARTBROKEN

The cost of being a have-a-go hero

The moment a once-proud nation was reduced to..

WAILS

Songwriters toast the British sausage

Carnivorous panda takes its revenge on man

Another body blow for boxing

Samoans quell moans

We bitch less, spit less, kiss less

U-TURN RULED OUT BY MAJOR

Hall's hot highlight

And he shoots...bipbipbip

Boys are the weaker sex in exams

'Granny rap' makes old age the rage in Japan

Commuters on slicks and bullhorns speed to work

NICK THE BOOTBOY JUDGE SAY CABBIES

The first symptom is dropping down dead

THE RED SPARROWS
Hot shot by Lisa, 9

1

MY FURY OVER RUGBY HATE!

I'm sorry, says judge who kicked a cabbie

My dark

days, by Seve

the champ

'I loved TV girl'

'I am living proof of the third sex'

He finally self-destructed

Anything you can do I can do whizzier

I wanted to scream at everybody, 'Help me'

We old men were in at the birth

£10,000: Price of our murdered girl's life

THE TIMES

THEATRE ROYAL, DRURY-LANE.
THIS EVENING, RULE A WIFE AND HAVE A WIFE.
Leon, Mr. Kean.
To which will be added, CHARLES THE BOLD.

THEATRE ROYAL, COVENT-GARDEN.
THIS EVENING, ISABELLA.
Isabella Miss O'Neill.
To which will be added, COMUS.

For the Benefit of Mr. BRANDON, Box-Book and House-keeper.
THEATRE-ROYAL, COVENT-GARDEN.
On FRIDAY, June 30. THE DUENNA.
Carlos, Mr. Sinclair, who will introduce ' Just like Love;'
Clara, Miss Stephens.
In the course of the evening, Black Ey'd Susan', and ' The
Storm,' by Mr. Incledon
With a FARCE and other ENTERTAINMENTS.
Tickets and places to be taken of Mr. Brandon, at the Box-office

LONDON, THURSDAY, JUNE 22, 1815.

OFFICIAL BULLETIN.

" DOWNING-STREET, JUNE 22, 1815.

"The Duke of WELLINGTON's Dispatch, dated Waterloo, the 19th of June, states, that on the preceding day BUONAPARTE attacked, with his whole force, the British line, supported by a corps of Prussians: which attack, after a long and sanguinary conflict, terminated in the complete Overthrow of the Enemy's Army, with the loss of ONE HUNDRED and FIFTY PIECES of CANNON and TWO EAGLES. During the night, the Prussians under Marshal BLUCHER, who joined in the pursuit of the enemy, captured SIXTY GUNS, and a large part of BUONAPARTE's BAGGAGE. The Allied Armies continued to pursue the enemy. Two French Generals were taken."

———

Such is the great and glorious result of those masterly movements by which the Hero of Britain met and frustrated the audacious attempt of the Rebel Chief. Glory to WELLINGTON, to our gallant Soldiers, and to our brave Allies ! BUONAPARTE's reputation has been wrecked, and his last grand stake has been lost in this tremendous conflict. TWO HUNDRED AND TEN PIECES OF CANNON captured in a single battle, put to the blush the boasting column of the Place de Vendome. Long and sanguinary, indeed, we fear, the conflict must have been; but the boldness of the Rebel Frenchmen was the boldness of despair, and conscience sate heavy on those arms which were raised against their Sovereign, against their oaths, and against the peace and happiness of their country. We confidently anticipate a great and immediate defection from the Rebel cause. We are aware that a great part of the French nation looked to the opening of this campaign with a superstitious expectation of success to a man, whom, though many of them hated, and many feared, all had been taught to look on as the first captain of the age. He himself went forth boasting in his strength, and still more in his talents.

Two hundred and ten pieces of cannon! When, where, or how is this loss to be repaired? Besides, what has become of his invincible guard, of his admired and dreaded cuirassiers? Again, we do not deny that these were good troops; but they were encountered by better. We shall be curious to learn with what degree of coolness, of personal courage, and self-possession, BUONAPARTE played this stake, on which he must have been well aware that his pretensions to Empire hung. It is clear that he retreated; nor are we prepared to hear that he fled with haste or cowardice; but we greatly suspect that he did not court an honourable death. We think his valour is of the calculating kind, and we do not attribute his surviving the abdication at Fontainebleau entirely to magnanimity.

To the official Bulletin we have as yet little to add. The dispatches, we understand, were brought by Major PERCY, Aide-de-Camp to the Duke of WELLINGTON; and we have heard, but we hope the statement is premature, that among the British slain was that gallant and estimable officer Sir THOMAS PICTON. But whoever fell on this glorious day cannot have fallen in vain. The fabric of rebellion is shaken to its base. Already, we hear, numerous desertions have taken place from the Rebel Standard; and soon, it is to be hoped, the perjured wretches NEY, and DESNOUETTES, and EXCELMANS, and LALLEMAND, and LABEDOYERE, and their accomplices in baseness and treason, will be left alone, as marks for the indignation of Europe, and just sacrifices to insulted French honour.

Those who attended minutely to the operations of the Stock Exchange yesterday, were persuaded that the news of the day before would be followed up by something still more brilliant and decisive. Omnium rose in the course of the day to 6 per cent. premium, and some houses generally supposed to possess the best information were among the purchasers. For our own parts, though looking forward with that confidence which we yesterday expressed, we frankly own this full tide of success was more than we had anticipated. We were very well satisfied that Mr. SUTTON's account, so far as it went, was correct,—that BUONAPARTE's grand plan had been frustrated, and that he had not only been prevented from penetrating between the English and Prussian armies, but forced to fall back again behind the Sambre. How far the Duke of WELLINGTON and Prince BLUCHER might have thought it prudent to pursue him, was a point on which we did not conceive ourselves warranted to form any decisive opinion from the evidence before us. We had no doubt that he would be harassed in his retreat, and perhaps ultimately be driven into his entrenched camp, or under the guns of his fortresses; but without some distinct official information, we repeat, that we could not have ventured to anticipate such a triumphant result as that on which we have now to congratulate our country and the world.

K

'WHITE WEAPONS.'
British Infantry's Dash and Daring.
By DR. T. MILLER MAGUIRE.
See Page FOUR.

Daily Express

Late War EDITION

"DAILY EXPRESS" FREE INSURANCE.
£1,000 at death
£1 10s. a week while disabled
£500 for loss of eye or limb
And other benefits
SEE PAGE 6.

NO. 5,128. LONDON, WEDNESDAY, SEPTEMBER 13, 1916. ONE HALFPENNY.

772ND DAY OF THE WAR.

Series of Great French Successes on the Somme Front.

GREAT ADVANCE BY THE FRENCH.

NEW LINE OF ENEMY TRENCHES CAPTURED IN 30 MINUTES.

MANY POSITIONS TAKEN.

DRAMATIC PUSH NEARER PERONNE.

Another dashing attack made yesterday by French troops north of the Somme resulted in splendid gains. It took place on a front of nearly four miles between Combles and the river, and at some points the advance was of considerable depth.

Hill 145, east of Le Forest, the Marrieres Wood, and the whole system of German trenches as far as the Bethune—Peronne road were taken, and the southern outskirts of the road are now held over a distance of a mile and a half. In addition, the French lines on Ridge 76, two miles north-west of Peronne, were pushed forward.

Up to last night 1,500 prisoners, including many officers, had been counted.

FIELD STREWN WITH DEAD.

TERRIBLE GERMAN LOSSES AT GINCHY.

BLINDED ARTILLERY

By PERCIVAL PHILLIPS.
"Daily Express" Special Correspondent.
WITH THE BRITISH ARMY IN THE FIELD, Sept 11.

The appearance of sixteen German balloons above the battle front beyond Ginchy to-day was in one respect a confession of defeat, for they signified that the enemy could no longer use the observation posts which overlooked our lines to the south and west.

They swung in the light breeze above the smoke-wreathed ruins of Ginchy and Guillemont, and the occupants attempted to direct a savage bombardment of the lost ground below, where British troops lay in new positions, with the German dead strewn about them, amid the wreckage of battle covering the fields and gullies over which they had advanced. Such counter-shelling was to be expected. The German guns, hastily concealed in new rearward positions, searched the ground they once occupied with a variety of explosives, and tried to find the British batteries which had come forward to harass them anew.

ROUNDING UP CIVILIANS.

DONE TO PROVE THAT NONE ESCAPE THE NET!

The following remarkable explanation of the "rounding up" of men at railway stations, music-halls, picture palaces, and football matches was issued last night by the Secretary of the War Office:—

Allegations are constantly being received at the War Office and in the commands to the effect that large numbers of young men have escaped registration and are consequently, unknown, to the military authorities, evading service. These allegations have been received from practically all the large centres of population, and it has been urged on the War Office that so long as these young men are permitted, through the laxity of the Recruiting Department, to remain in civil life, it is grossly unfair to draw on the older groups and classes.

In order to test the accuracy of these allegations, an examination of certificates of exemption in possession of men of military age has recently been undertaken, and these so-called "rounds up" have been carried out in a number of districts. So far the result has been to demonstrate that in the sections of the country which have been tested the allegations are without foundation.

If this was the sole object of setting such ponderous machinery in motion it has been fully achieved, for among the thousands of men who have been cross-examined scarcely a score of slackers have been found. It is to be presumed that the raids will now be abandoned.

William Pitt, aged forty-eight, who was said to have refused to answer questions when captured in a raid, was fined £1 at Tottenham yesterday for being "drunk and riotous."

A raid on a circus tent at Camberley had to be abandoned because all the lights suddenly went out. Raids on two places of amusement at Portsmouth proved fruitless, as have several raids on music-halls, picture palaces, and parks at Bath.

NATIONAL TRIBUTE TO THE AIRMAN V.C.

GIFT OF ORNAMENTAL IRONWORK FOR THE MONUMENT.

HOW A PUBLIC DEBT MAY BE FULFILLED.

No one can tell how many lives and what amount of property were saved from destruction by Lieutenant W. L. Robinson's splendid deed in foiling the attempt of Zeppelin L 21 to raid London on Sunday, September 3. It is impossible to state where the bombs might have fallen, but every resident and business firm of the metropolis and the surrounding suburbs is under a deep debt of gratitude to the heroic airman.

It is not only Londoners, however, who benefited by the bringing down of the airship. Had the Zeppelin escaped it is impossible to say what provincial towns it might not have attacked on its homeward journey or on some other occasion.

The public debt of gratitude to Lieutenant Robinson, V.C., can best be expressed by a contribution to the "Daily Express" fund to erect a monument on the site where the Zeppelin fell a flaming mass of wreckage.

DOUBLE DEFEAT FOR THE BULGARS.

FRENCH CAPTURE TWO MILES OF TRENCHES: BRITISH SUCCESS ON THE STRUMA.

GREEK CABINET CRISIS.

BALKAN FRONT.—The Allies' push on the Salonika front in the Balkans was extended and developed yesterday. Lieut.-General Milne, the British commander-in-chief, reports that the Bulgars suffered severely in the fighting which followed the crossing of the Struma by the British, and that our offensive has been extended to the Doiran front, where our guns are very active.

West of the Vardar the French have won an important success, capturing two miles of Bulgar trenches and taking some prisoners.

RUMANIAN FRONT.—The Rumanians report the conquest in twelve days of 7,500 square miles of Hungarian territory in Transylvania. On their southern front they are bombarding Rustchuk, the great Danube port.

GREECE.—The Greek Premier, M. Zaimis, has resigned. His action is said to be due to domestic difficulties.

SETS THE SEAL ON ANY MEAL
H·P SAUCE

DAILY HERALD

This is the Gin
Gordon's
Stands Supreme

No. 7672 MONDAY, SEPTEMBER 16, 1940 ONE PENNY

175 NAZI PLANES DOWN

Buckingham Palace Is bombed third time

BY JOHN SLEE
"Daily Herald" Reporter

Two bombs were deliberately dropped on Buckingham Palace during yesterday's first raid.

They fell into the Queen's apartment and on to the lawns of the palace, but did not explode.

One crashed through the tapestry room used by the Queen as a drawing-room and tore a hole in the ceiling.

The King and Queen were not in residence at the time, and only a skeleton staff of servants and others was in the Palace. They were all in the basement shelters and there were no casualties

The Palace A.R.P. staff and police dealt with a few incendiary bombs which fell in the grounds and started a few small fires. They were quickly put out.

"It was obvious this plane had been told to bomb the Palace," said one observer. "Yet no sooner had he unloaded than he was chased by our fighters, who immediately opened fire"

This was the third time the Palace had been bombed.

One wing of a raider, blown to pieces over Central London yesterday, fell on the roof of a building. Other pictures of wrecked Nazi planes are on Page Three.

DOWN OVER CITY

RAF Triumphs In Biggest Air Battles Of War

GOERING'S AIR FORCE HAD LOST 175 MACHINES UP TO TEN O'CLOCK LAST NIGHT FOLLOWING A DAY WHICH SAW FOUGHT THE FIERCEST AIR BATTLES OF THE WAR. FIGHTERS BROUGHT DOWN 171 AND A.A. FIRE FOUR.

Thirty British fighters were lost, but ten of the pilots are safe. The total of enemy aircraft destroyed is now 2,158.

Soon after the fourth Alert of the day, at 8.10, the A.A. barrage began to spread its protecting mantle of steel and fire over the capital.

Just before 3 a.m. to-day the following Air Ministry and Ministry of Home Security communiqué announced:

"Early yesterday afternoon a large force of enemy aircraft crossed the coast of Kent and attempted to force a way through to the London area.

"Anti-aircraft defences went into action, and the invaders were intercepted and heavily engaged at the coast by our fighters.

"In the ensuing battle, which ranged over Kent from the coast to the Thames estuary, heavy losses were inflicted on the invaders.

BROKEN UP

"The main formation was broken up and many of the enemy were chased back across the Channel.

"Some enemy aircraft, however, broke away and flew over the Medway district and the Thames Estuary. Others forced their way through to the London area, where they were successfully engaged by fresh squadrons.

"Bombs were dropped at several points in and around the London area, and at many points in South-East England. Many small fires were caused, and houses are reported to have been damaged in several districts.

STOP PRESS

BERLIN HAS TWO ALARMS

Berlin had a 27-minute air raid alarm, from 11.30 to 11.57 last night.

Later a second air raid alarm sent Berliners to their shelters for half an hour. It was stated that no bombs were dropped.

It was the first time since the start of the war that they had had their sleep disturbed twice in one night.

BOMB SCARE IN NEW YORK

NEW YORK, Sunday.

Traffic between Brooklyn and Manhattan, over the Williamsburg Bridge, was suspended for 40 minutes this afternoon while the police examined a package, which it was feared might contain a bomb.

Experts plunged the package in oil and carried it to the river bank.—British United Press.

RAIDERS CHASED BACK TO THE CHANNEL

THE two main bodies of raiders over the London area yesterday received such a gruelling as never before.

Spitfire and Hurricane squadrons, many of them veterans in London defence, fought them over the Kent coast as they came in, fought them over Maidstone and Canterbury, fought them above the Medway and Thames Estuary.

Many they turned away. The survivors they fought again over London itself, squadron after squadron of fighters flying fresh into action.

Finally they chased them back again and out over the Channel.

A squadron of Hurricanes which destroyed nine of the enemy began its fight over London and ended up over the cliffs of Hastings.

Another chased a group of bombers from the Thames at Hammersmith to Beachy Head, shooting down five of their number on the way.

TWO ITALIAN PLANES RAID LONDON

By a "Daily Herald" Reporter

TWO Italian planes took part in the midday raid on London yesterday.

"I am not suggesting they were Italian," said a Mr. Plasted, who watched them through glasses. "I'm telling you they were Italian."

RAF PUTS GOERING IN SHADE

GERMAN air raids on this country appear small compared with the fierce offensive the RAF is carrying out against Germany's invasion bases.

Foreign reports state that the Navy is taking part in the attacks.

Wave after wave of RAF bomber formations are, hour after hour, day after day, keeping up a continuous bombardment of shipping and troop concentrations at Channel and North Sea ports.

On the other hand, German mass raids on London rarely last more than an hour, and seldom are there more than two in a day.

Single planes or small formations do the rest of the Nazi raiding.

Bigger Formations

The RAF it became apparent last night, has during the past 24 hours dealt Germany one of the heaviest blows since the war started.

Its bombers, in bigger formations than ever before, have smashed away with tremendous fury at the enemy.

The Air Ministry told last night how large forces of British bombers ranged on Saturday night and early yesterday over Germany, France, Belgium and Holland, systematically seeking out and breaking up the German High Command's invasion machine.

Flying through appalling weather—aircraft were struck by lightning, radio aerials were burned off in violent electric storms, and many machines were "iced up"—the raiders struck heavily at the German "front line" in the ports.

(Continued on Back Page, Col. 3.)

L

The Daily Poſt.

FRIDAY, April 22, 1720.

Paris, April 24.

YESTERDAY in the Morning a Swiſs, who had been formerly a Soldier, came to the Bank to receive the Money upon a Bank Bill, which was known to be one of the Bills which was taken from the unfortunate Footman, who belong'd to Monſ. de Buſca, who was aſſaſſinated and barbarouſly murder'd ſome Time ago. The Fellow was immediately ſtopt and ſeiz'd upon, and being examined by the Lieutenant Criminel, and threaten'd with the Torture, declar'd, that he had the Bill of a Soldier of the Foot Guards, and nam'd one Fenelot, who he ſaid lodg'd or quarter'd in ſuch a Place as he alſo nam'd. The Soldier was immediately order'd to be ſeiz'd, and was taken in the Place where the Swiſs directed. It is not doubted but by one or other of thoſe two, that barbarous Murder may be detected, and the Offender brought to Juſtice. There is a Surgeon's Apprentice ſuſpected to have been an Accomplice in what was done, and a Prieſt; but they have been fled long enough to have ſecur'd themſelves. If theſe are convicted, they will be made terrible Examples; for the Murders and Robberies lately committed in this City have been intollerable for Number, and ſome of them horrid in their Manner, more than ordinary.

Theſe Murders and Robberies have been ſo dreadful here, that People are afraid to ſtir out of Doors after 'tis dark, or to walk out into the Fields adjoyning to the City, but with very good Company, moſt of them have been ſuppoſed to be committed upon the Perſons of ſuch People as have had Bank Bills and Eaſt-India Company Actions about them; and tho' abundance of Bodies have been found in the Seine, and in common Shores and private Places, yet there are many miſſing too that have not been found at all; and what is yet more ſtrange, not one of theſe Murderers have been apprehended, or indeed diſcover'd, except that which was committed by the Count de Horn and his Accomplice, who were broke upon the Wheel for it.

Stick on a plaster: kick the habit

Will Cadbury mean real change?

OFF MY BACK, BRUNO

Who's afraid of a Lib/Lab pact?

If couples can be selfish, why can't I?

Why try to whisper if you're not the quiet type?

At last, music to Europe's ears

When giving is all a matter of time

Bring in Baker, Bush told

STOP THE PLANE..IT'S FALLING TO PIECES

Don't panic, figures need not be meaningless

TIME TO PAY UP

THE FURRY FRIENDS WHO COULDN'T FACE DEEP FREEZE BRITAIN

Who'd be a monkey?

GET FELL IN – TO LIVE ON AN ARMY BASE!

Go on, give yourself a lift!

What do we care about – buildings or bodies?

How young riders can learn to be safe in the saddle

'Imagine being born a write-off'

Why crack down on refugees who aren't coming?

Perspiration problem? No sweat

Car sticker maniacs: why on earth do they Do It?

SMASH HIT! ANGRY POP STAR PUNCHES TV PHIL

UK postal service 'a benchmark' for EC standards

British child care 'worst in Europe despite tax relief'

Lancashire's spot of good fortune

Tories 'horrified' by party deficit

Golden reign of King William

Carlton ahead after video successes

Top scorer Wright the right reserve

Radiation fear over sports plan for lake

Seabrook the unsung hero

EC polarised on budget proposals

Not a sausage for hungry Belgian force

Busy lines on secret Kremlin phone network

BODY SHOP POTIONS STILL MAGICAL

P ## SCHOOLS TO REPORT KIDS ON A 'RACIST FORM'

Friendly fire pilots to face Congress

Ratners to cut Watches' sale price

British Coal to increase pensions

Students to compete in 'knowledge Olympics'

Fowler to shake up staff at Tory HQ

Street Art to combat graffiti

Reynolds to fight on as appeal fails

Tajik opposition to share power

Victory in cash card case

★★★★

by IAN FLETCHER
Consumer Correspondent

A BANK customer who claimed money from his account disappeared through a cash dispenser yesterday won in the first case of its kind.

Outdoor instructor John Allan, 28, sued the Bank of Scotland and won compensation from his account.

The missing cash had been withdrawn with a card, leaving Allan short of the right transaction "hole-in-the-wall" machine.

The bank refused to compensate him and the economic "hole-in-the-wall" case. An out-of-court settle-

ment was reached after the Consumers' Association backed his claim.

They had planned to call evidence from a computer expert to back up the case. Allan claimed, show the cash machines could go wrong.

But Barclays are director David Tench said: "The terms are confidential but Mr Allan is happy.

"These machines are very, very rarely fallible but this is the first such machine failure in a very considerable dilemma. Maybe we will have to

here to get us out of the way. Some of the natural homes have been boarded up but we will all know that.

Neighbour Paula Scotney, 32, added: "I have seen council houses empty around this city, but they have left us down here.

"Our children have been playing around but now the feel air that it is not safe and now they should go an special doctors.

"Why wasn't something done before? This has turned our lives upside down.

Portsmouth is one of the nation's "hotspots" for asbestos disease, chest expert Dr Sherwood Bosker said last night. It is also on the increase in many other ports, including Plymouth, Liverpool, Southampton and Chatham, Kent, where asbestos was used to insulate ships and prevent burning.

Dr Bodge said the risk of disease was slight. "He added: "There has always been a lot of sickness and diarrhoea around here among the children but we have put it down to the weather.

"Now we never suspected for one minute that it was anything to do with asbestos. Some of them or the dangers. If I feel we were just dumped down

queue up again for our money and none of us will like that."

● Credit card holders will soon be writing out a cheque instead of flashing their plastic in stores.

The changes are to introduce distinctive cheque books for eight million customers throughout the UK.

A spokesman said: "This can see the cheques in places can't accept credit cards.

"This will help fill the gap.

Families ordered out of time-bomb asbestos estate

by CLIVE NELSON and NICKI POPE

FIFTY-SEVEN families were last night ordered to abandon their homes within 24 hours after deadly asbestos was discovered on a council estate.

They were asked to have immediate medical checks but a leading chest expert warned they face a health "timebomb" which could explode in 20 to 30 years' time.

Dangerously high levels of asbestos, including the most dangerous blue asbestos, which causes lung disease and cancer, were discovered after soil samples taken from the Lumsden Road estate in Portsmouth, Hampshire.

Council housing chairman Brian Pope said: "It is a precaution but we're sure to safeguard them. We wanted to act as quickly as possible.

Residents claimed last night that they had been "kept in the dark" by council officials.

Mother-of-five Pat Taylor, 35, said: "We knew this was something in some areas but we never made the wave and but we were not told what they were for. Now, we are told to get out within 24 hours.

She added: "There has always been a lot of sickness and diarrhoea around here among the children but we have put it down to the weather...

Hurd backs November election

FOREIGN Secretary Douglas Hurd indicated last night that a November election is on the cards.

He said the party had turned against Labour and is moving towards the Government.

"Labour's nuclear tide of optimism which believes that it is John Major who suffers the right leadership for our country," Mr Hurd told Tory Forces in Wales, Oxfordshire.

It is the lull in the economy and failure of the Labour party in changing people's views, he added. "Labour offers no choice of a leader without a credible party, or a party without a credible leader."

The Poll debate: Page 6

Yeltsin ill with heart problem

RUSSIA'S president Boris Yeltsin was last night said to be suffering from a heart problem.

He added he was going ahead with a planned additional trip to the Russian parliament after being taken ill in recent days.

His secretary denied earlier reports he had been taken to hospital from the parliament building, but admitted he had taken the day off work.

He said: "He has a minor heart problem and went home to rest.

The secretary said that Mr Yeltsin would be going ahead with a planned additional trip to the Russian parliament today. Sources said other items on his agenda would remain unchanged.

Nuclear subs danger alert

MAJOR structural defects aboard Britain's nuclear-powered hunter submarines have been hidden from MPs, a former atomic safety chief claims.

The fleet is crippled by reactor leaks and affected vessels are being kept in locked vessels without special permission.

At least two of the submarines have been refused safety certificates and the others with discovered safety chief claims Reginald Farmer, former UK Atomic Authority safety chief on ITV's This Week tonight.

RAF jets put on desert war alert

From Page 1

Saddam is resisting. There is concern he believes the West has lost the battle in Iraq because of the breakup of the Soviet Union and the Yugoslav crisis.

Talks are still underway with representatives of the UN in the hopes of reaching agreements over warfare since disagreements and averting new hostilities.

A US official said: "The resolution makes quite clear that the Iraqis are in no position to do anything.

General John Galvin, Supreme Allied Commander in Europe, confirmed in an informal military television rehearsal manoeuvres in the Gulf was possible.

White House spokesman Marlin Fitzwater said President Bush had conferred on the Gulf crisis.

Power chief in pay row

NWCB's shareholders lashed out at an electric company's chief yesterday when he refused to disclose his salary.

Norweb chairman Ken Harvey defended directors' pay at the annual meeting in Manchester.

He said: "Jays are salaries which it is not essential if we are to retain our directors."

The annual report showed 50 directors in the £60,135 last year.

It said he believed it to be around 60 per cent.

CHAMP DROPS DEAD AT MR MUSCLES CONTEST

'Heart attack' tragedy as Andy, 23, limbers up

By MIRROR REPORTER

TOP musician Andy Hornby collapsed and died minutes before he was due to compete in the Mr England bodybuilding contest.

Sixteen stone Andy, 23, died in his girlfriend's arms after being taken ill as he limbered up in a corridor. It is thought he suffered a massive heart attack. Three other competitors. But he collapsed as girlfriend Theresa Thornton helped him out of the changing room and he was rushed to the Gateshead Leisure Centre, Tyne and Wear on Saturday.

The tragedy stunned an audience of 1,500 at the Gateshead Leisure Centre, Tyne and Wear on Saturday.

Girlfriend Theresa said Andy was very popular. "Andy was very popular with the show. Everyone wanted to go on with the show when he was on.

"But everyone was very subdued. Everyone who knew him, felt his death deeply.

"Last night Theresa was too distraught to talk at the home she shared with Andy in Tyne and Wear.

But his father Ken, 50, dismissed suggestions that Andy, a milkman, had been taking drugs to pump up his body building.

He said: "He lived for the sport. He trained hard for this contest for six months.

"I've no way he would have jeopardised all that.

Andy's mother June added: "At least he died knowing that he had died his last competition.

"He was a fantastically devastated.

JACKO SETS UP JOKE WEDDING

ZANY Michael Jackson got such a kick out of Liz Taylor's wedding that he is now arranging one of his own.

Startled Brooke, 26, said she wanted to marry the sex god, but Jacko, 33, told her it would not be a real wedding.

Giggling Brooke agreed to be the bride – probably at Christmas.

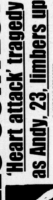

GROOM: Jacko

"It's not an ordinary loss that most people loss in the 12 weeks before dying. We tried everything to improve the young man.

An inquest is expected to be opened today.

"If you are not careful you can put a tremendous strain on your heart. Sometimes the heart can't take the pressure.

Four years ago Andy weighed just under 16st. He developed a love of bottles and a gambling habit. He was determined to spend my money to my career.

"We have no comment about that."

SHILTON WRANGLE OVER HOME LOAN

By CHRISTIAN DYSEN

MILLIONAIRE soccer star Peter Shilton talked last night about the mortgage difficulties that have left him behind with payments on his luxury home.

But admits it was me responsible which should have been made over some payments and he there could be a court appearance over the missed payments.

He said: "I will admit there are problems but nothing more." I have paid the money owed and I feel I think has been sorted out.

Asked about his love of horses and a gambling problem, the former England goalkeeper who earns an estimated £1m a year with Second Division

keeper once star Peter Shilton now owns three horses. His business interests make him one of the richest footballers in history.

Derby County tracker home racing fan and his boss's gambling and the lover life to be full for

LETTER: Shilton

A Derby County reader of Peter Shilton's in Hampshire.

What to look for in newspapers

Format

National daily newspapers fall into two categories according to their format (or size): **broadsheets** – large-format papers like *The Times*, the *Independent* and the *Guardian*; and **tabloids** – small-format papers like the *Daily Mirror*, the *Daily Express* and the *Sun*.

Content

Newspapers are bought by a variety of people, who read them for many different reasons. One person might buy a paper mainly for amusement, another might want a paper which deals in depth with the latest political events. Tabloids often combine news of current affairs with items which are more light-hearted, such as 'gossip' columns and features on people's lives. Broadsheets, on the other hand, tend to have more text in relation to pictures, and feature largely news and current affairs.

Layout

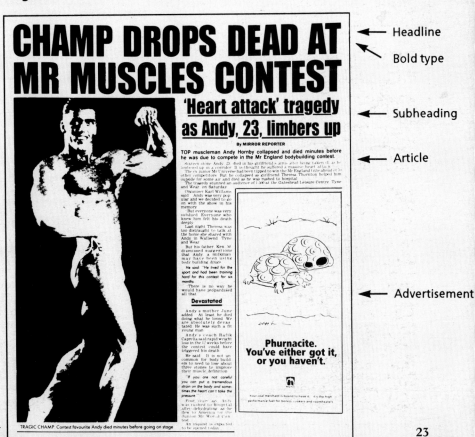

← Headline

← Bold type

← Subheading

← Article

← Advertisement

Caption →

↑ Column

Activities to focus on the use of headlines

One

*Text A is a page from the **Daily Mirror**, 9 October 1991. It contains nine news stories and one advertisement. There are nine headlines, and even the advertisement has something like a headline.*

✪ **EXPLORATION**

✪ Which story is given the biggest headline? Why?
✪ Are there any subheadings? What are they for?
✪ Are there any headlines that do not appear at the top of the story?
✪ In how many different ways are the headlines set out? (Compare **EASY COME, EASY GO** with **ANIMAL PLEA** and **RAIN RAP FOR SPAIN**.)
✪ How many different typefaces are used on this page? Do they vary within the same story as well as between stories?

ACTIVITY 1

Writers of headlines appear to enjoy playing with words. Their jokes may not seem especially funny. How many verbal jokes can you find on this page?

ACTIVITY 2

In addition to headlines, newspapers usually put captions under the pictures. Look at the captions here. What do they have in common? The picture of the motorcyclist does not have an obvious caption. Write one along the lines of the others.

ACTIVITY 3

There are at least five places in the advertisement where the typeface is much heavier, or bolder, than the rest. Why has this been done?

ACTIVITY 4

Headlines have to be brief, which means that the choice of words is all important. Choose some words or phrases from the headlines in Text A and say why they have caught your attention.

Text B is taken from **Today**, *28 October 1991.*

ACTIVITY 1

Look carefully at the words used in the headlines in Text B. Select one or two words that seem to you to have a strong effect on the reader. Use the same words in headlines you have invented. Do they still have the same effect?

ACTIVITY 2

Collect two other daily papers and compare some of the headlines with those in Text B. Make a note of similarities and differences. Which headlines interest or please you, and which do you dislike?

ACTIVITY 3

The subeditor has the job of creating a newspaper's headlines each day. Draw up a list of advice to subeditors on what makes a good headline.

ACTIVITY 4

Write a definition of the word 'headline'. When you have done this, compare your definition with those in at least three different dictionaries.

Three

*Text C comes from the **Daily Mirror**, 28 October 1991: the same day as the preceding text from **Today**.*

ACTIVITY

All the headlines have been removed from Text C. Imagine you are the subeditor for the day. Read the news stories and write headlines you think are suitable.

Meet in groups of up to six to make editorial decisions about which headlines best suit each story. Each group should swap their headlines with those of another group and then vote for the ones they think should have been published. This will make sure you are not judging your own headlines and you will also find out what other people think about your writing.

As a group you may decide that some of the chosen headlines need changing slightly to get them just right. (Think about the sort of advice you gave to subeditors in the last activity.) The headlines actually published on the day are given on page 22.

Four

*Text D comes from **Today**, 19 September 1991. Again, the headlines for that day have been removed.*

ACTIVITY 1

Write down what you think the actual headlines might have been, then swap your headlines with someone else's. For each article, discuss which of your two headlines you would have chosen if you'd been a subeditor for *Today*. The headlines actually published are given on page 22.

ACTIVITY 2

Discuss the following questions in a group or with a partner:

How did you judge what makes a suitable headline?
What did you argue about when choosing the headlines?
How sensational were the headlines you decided to publish?
How do you think your headlines would affect the people they are written about?

Text E is a collection of headlines which are all written in a very similar way.

⊙ **EXPLORATION**

⊙ Read the headlines aloud as though they were the news headlines on radio or TV.
⊙ Would people talk like this in everyday conversation?
⊙ What is the similarity between the headlines?

ACTIVITY 1

Write down three items of news about your school in the style of these headlines. Now imagine you are telling a friend the same three pieces of news and write down what you would say. Limit yourself to one sentence for each piece of news. List the differences between your three headlines and your three sentences.

The special style of the headlines in Text E is achieved by stringing together two or more nouns in what are called **noun phrases**. *In headlines, phrases consisting of three nouns in a row are very common. For example,* **COMPACT DISC DEALS** *starts with a three-noun phrase. Rows, or strings, of four nouns do occur but are less common. An example of a four-noun phrase is* **RAIL BRIDGE PLUNGE HORROR**.

ACTIVITY 2

Collect some old newspapers and explore the headlines. Make a written note of any that sound like the examples given in Text E. Look for a two-noun phrase, eg **MOTORBIKE MADNESS** . . .; a three-noun phrase, eg **BUILDERS' JOBS GLOOM** . . .; a four-noun phrase; and a five-noun phrase. See who can collect the most four-noun and five-noun phrases – they are the most difficult to find!

ACTIVITY 3

The following headlines have been made up in the style of those in Text E. Write the news stories that could follow them. Use no more than six sentences. Tell the main piece of news in the first sentence, describe the events in the next sentences, and make the last sentence a comment from someone who was interviewed. Use direct speech in the last sentence, such as "We're glad it's all over," said Mrs Pearce, the lollipop lady.

SWEETS BAN THREAT ANGERS PUPILS AT NORTHFIELDS SCHOOL

GLUE FACTORY SOCCER TEAM COMES UNSTUCK

POP CONCERT DEATH ENQUIRY BLAMES FAULTY WIRING

SPACE WALK DOG MYSTERY SOLVED BY SCHOOLGIRL ASTRONOMER

MIRACLE BIKE CRASH HERO RETURNS TO GRAND PRIX RACING

Six

Use Texts A and B for this activity, as well as newspapers you have collected.

> ❂ **EXPLORATION**
>
> A newspaper headline usually summarises the story that follows it. Compare the headlines in Texts A and B with the opening sections of their stories:
>
> ❂ Which words in the headlines are repeated in the opening paragraphs?
> ❂ What sort of information is given in the opening paragraphs but not mentioned in the headlines?

ACTIVITY 1

Search through other newspapers and ask yourself how often the headline summarises, or states, the main point of the story. Does it happen every time? What sort of information is used in the headlines and what is left out?

ACTIVITY 2

Look at one or two stories in Texts A and B and write alternative headlines that present the news in a different light. Your new versions should make sense, but make sure you do not change what actually happened in the stories.

*Text F (i) is a front page from the **Independent**. Text F (ii) shows headlines that appeared in the **Independent** during one week in May 1992.*

✪ **EXPLORATION**

The **subject** is usually the person who does the action of a verb. Every headline except one in Text F (i) begins with its subject closely followed by the **main verb**. All these verbs are in the **active** form because the subject is doing the action of the verb.

✪ Make a list of all the subjects in these headlines, followed by each main verb. For example:

Subject	Main verb
Clarke	Rejects

✪ The **structure** of the headline LABOUR WARNED ON UNION CASH is different. How would you describe the difference?

This structure puts the verb in a **passive** form, which means that the action of the verb is done to the subject, not by the subject. 'Labour' were warned by someone else; they did not do the warning. Who did? Read the story and rewrite the headline so that it says who gave the warning.

ACTIVITY 1

All the headlines apart from LABOUR WARNED ON UNION CASH use verbs in the active form. Rewrite all these headlines so that they are in the passive. For example, CLARKE REJECTS CALL FOR REFORM AT DARTMOOR becomes CALL FOR REFORM AT DARTMOOR REJECTED BY CLARKE. What difference does this make to your understanding?

ACTIVITY 2

If headlines are read aloud, one after another, they can sound dramatic. Write down all the *Independent* headlines in the form of a newsreader's script (radio or TV) so that a newsreader could read them out after announcing, 'Here are the news headlines . . .' You need not follow the order in which they are printed on the front page. You may think, for example, that the news about President Bush's pledge to save forests is more important than prison reform or Scottish devolution. If you wish, you can change the headlines to make some active and some passive.

ACTIVITY 3

Look at Text F (ii). Find the verb used in all but one of the headlines –
it looks as though it was the verb of the week for the *Independent*
subeditors! Why is this verb so useful for news reporters?

Eight

*The headlines in Text G show quite strongly what the subeditor
wants us to think about the people involved in the stories.*

✪ EXPLORATION

✪ Which headlines seem sympathetic and approving, which
   unsympathetic or disapproving? Put them into two groups:
   sympathetic and unsympathetic.
✪ How did you decide which were which? Was it the use of a
   particular word, or something else?

ACTIVITY 1

What changes would you make to some of the headlines in Text G in
order to make the reader react differently? How, for example, could
you make an unsympathetic headline more sympathetic?

ACTIVITY 2

Think of some recent local or national events and write headlines for
them that are strongly sympathetic or unsympathetic. For example:

(BLANK) SCHOOL CHESS TEAM ANNIHILATES ALL OPPOSITION

TEACHER UNFAIRLY DISMISSED (OR) TEACHER FINALLY SACKED

LOCAL YOBS DESTROY CHILDREN'S PLAYGROUND

MAGNIFICENT CHARITY EFFORT BY YEAR 9 PUPILS

Nine

Text H illustrates some of the ways in which headline writers use language to grab the reader's attention.

> ⚙ **EXPLORATION**
>
> ⚙ Which headlines are difficult to say out loud?
> ⚙ Which headlines use ideas to shock the reader?

ACTIVITY 1

How many different kinds of wordplay can you find in these headlines? Group your examples under different headings. For example, one heading might be 'letters that are repeated' and under this would go **ANOTHER BODY BLOW FOR BOXING**. Collect your own examples of headlines that 'play' with words to produce an effect and add them to the ones from Text H.

ACTIVITY 2

Look through some newspapers and see if you can rewrite some of the headlines in a more eye-catching (or 'ear-catching') way. Write down the original headlines in one column and your improved version beside them.

Ten

Text I gives some examples of pronouns and possessive adjectives in use.

> *Pronouns (eg I, you, she) and their possessive adjectives (my, your, her) are words that are easy to take for granted. We use them a great deal. Here are the complete sets:*
>
> *Pronouns: I, me, you, he, him, she, her, we, us, they, them, it.*
> *Possessive adjectives: my, your, her, his, our, their, its.*

ACTIVITY 1

List the pronouns and possessive adjectives used in Text I. Which pronoun is used most? Which possessive adjective is used most? Why do you think subeditors use these particular ones so often in headlines? What effect do they have on the reader? Do any of the other pronouns and possessive adjectives have a similar effect?

ACTIVITY 2

Explore some other newspapers and find more examples of pronouns and possessive adjectives. How often are they used to report what somebody has said?

Eleven

Texts J, K, and L are taken from historic war reports.

> ✪ **EXPLORATION**
>
> ✪ Summarise the main events in each report and give each summary a modern headline.
> ✪ Remember that your headline should state the main point of the report. Look at the opening paragraph of the report for this information.

ACTIVITY 1

The account of the Battle of Waterloo (Text J) appeared in *The Times*, 22 June 1815. It was the main story of that year (let alone that day), yet it did not appear on the front page. For many years the front page of a newspaper was devoted to advertisements and public notices. Pictures did not appear in newspapers until much more recently. Compare the Battle of Waterloo account with the more familiar layout of the First World War account (Text K) and the Battle of Britain reports (Text L). What differences are there in the layout and typefaces used?

ACTIVITY 2

From the evidence of the three reports written between 1815 and 1940, make a list of features you feel are common to war reporting. Look especially at the language used (eg words and phrases). Can you find any evidence of bias in the reporting? How might the French have reported Waterloo, or the Germans the Battle of Britain?

ACTIVITY 3

Newspapers in any age contain many reports of war, or rumours of war somewhere in the world. Find as many examples of war reporting as you can. Cut out or write down the headlines and keep a record of the date and the name of the papers in which they appeared. You could look at what nouns, verbs and adjectives are used; at how feelings and bias are expressed; or at the reporting of comments made, or said to have been made, by the soldiers, sailors or airmen. Using your examples, make a plan for a wall display on the language of war reporting.

ACTIVITY 4

Choose four war headlines from any newspapers and write them down with a space between each. Now find four headlines that tell of good news and write these between your war headlines. Your writing will now begin to look like a poem. Read it and re-arrange the headlines until you are satisfied with the effect. Add an opening and a closing line of your own. Think carefully about what you want the last line to say to the reader. Finally, think of a title.

Twelve

Text M is from the **Daily Post***, Friday, 22 April 1720. It is a crime report from a Paris correspondent and has all the ingredients of a modern TV thriller.*

ACTIVITY 1

Rewrite the report in the style of modern journalism. Start by deciding which paper you are writing for, eg the *Daily Mirror* or the *Independent*, and so on. Do you feel that the gruesome punishment suggested in the final sentence is too out of date for a modern account? Omit it if you wish. Note that you will need to modernise some of the language.

ACTIVITY 2

When you have written your modernised version, decide on a suitable headline. You should also decide on which photographs you want. Pretend your photographer has been lucky or enterprising enough to get some good ones.

ACTIVITY 3

Crime reports have been regular features since the early days of newspapers. Collect some examples from modern papers and explore the ways in which headlines make the story as exciting or as sensational as possible.

What makes crime such a popular topic in newspapers? Using the evidence you have collected from popular papers, discuss how the bare facts may be turned into 'a good story'.

ACTIVITY 4

Collect crime headlines and stories from broadsheet papers like the *Guardian*, the *Independent*, or *The Times*. How do their crime headlines and reports differ from those in the tabloid papers?

ACTIVITY 5

Look at a variety of papers for the same period of time, for example one or two weeks. Compare how the headline for one crime story is treated by different newspapers.

Thirteen

Text N contains a selection of headlines.

✪ EXPLORATION

There are four types of sentence. Each one is used to communicate in a different way:

Statements tell you something: 'The temperature today is 30 °C.'
Questions ask you something: 'Have you switched on the fan?'
Commands tell you to do something: 'Switch on the fan, please.'
Exclamations call or cry out: 'Phew! What a heatwave!'

✪ Which of these types of sentence is not used very much in writing but does occur quite often in speech? Why do you think this is so?

ACTIVITY 1

Look at the headlines in Text N and decide what type of sentence they are. You could discuss this in groups.

ACTIVITY 2

Read through a page from any paper. How frequently does each type of sentence occur? Make a table with four columns and mark a line in one column every time a particular sentence type is used. You should discover an order of frequency. Compare your findings with the rest of your class.

Text O contains a selection of headlines, all with a missing ingredient!

⊘ EXPLORATION

The first headline in Text O is made up of two parts: an **exclamation**, SMASH HIT!, followed by a statement, ANGRY POP STAR PUNCHES TV PHIL. In this example, the verb ('punches') is actually used on the page; it is **explicit**. But headlines often leave the verb out; it is then only in the reader's mind and is said to be **implicit** or **implied**.

⊘ Read the headlines in Text O and find the 'missing' verb in each case. The word that is often missing is a word like 'is' or 'are'. For example, BRITISH CHILD CARE (IS) WORST IN EUROPE.

ACTIVITY 1

Verbs are normally described as 'doing' or 'action' words and the many thousands contained in an English dictionary are just that. But the two most frequently used verbs are not such obvious action words. They are the verbs *be* (*am, is, are, was, were, been* are all parts of this verb) and *have* (*has, had* are both parts of this verb). Look through the news stories you have studied so far and find five sentences using parts of the verb *be* and five using parts of the verb *have*. Can you turn any of the sentences using the verb *be* into 'headlines' by leaving out the verb? (This won't always be possible!)

ACTIVITY 2

The verbs *be* and *have* can be used:

- on their own
    She *was* in Year 8.
- with another verb
    We *have broken* the world record.
- with each other
    I *am having* a really good time.

If they are used in front of another verb or in front of each other they are called **auxiliary** (or 'helping') verbs. In the examples above *have* and *am* are auxiliary verbs. Look again at the sentences you found in Activity 1. For each sentence say whether the verbs *be* and *have* are being used as auxiliary verbs or not.

The headlines in Text P all use a particular part of the verb, the infinitive.

> ✪ **EXPLORATION**
>
> ✪ Look at the verbs in the headlines in Text P and decide what the verbs, which are all **infinitives**, have in common.

ACTIVITY 1

All the headlines in Text P have a missing or implied verb(s), for example FOWLER (IS PLANNING) TO SHAKE UP STAFF AT TORY HQ. But, by using the same words as in the headline and adding different verbs before the infinitive, you could invent sentences that don't describe the future. For example:

FOWLER HAS FORGOTTEN TO SHAKE UP STAFF AT TORY HQ.

FOWLER WENT TO SHAKE UP STAFF AT TORY HQ.

Take one of the headlines in Text P and see how many different meanings you can create by using different verbs before the infinitive.

ACTIVITY 2

In Activity 1 you saw that in ordinary language the infinitive on its own doesn't tell us about the **time** something happened. The verb that comes before the infinitive tells us about this. But headlines commonly use the infinitive on its own to point to what is likely to happen in the future. Invent some headlines of your own that use the infinitive in this way. Think of possible events at home or at school.

General activities on headlines

The Headline Game

1   Three or more players can play the Headline Game.

2   You will need a dictionary, some scrap paper, a pen or pencil each and a clock or watch to time two-minute rounds.

3   Nominate one player to keep the score.

4   Decide how many rounds you will play. (One round will probably take about three minutes in total to play and score.)

5   When it is their go, each player in turn thinks of a sequence of four letters and shows them to the other players. They then act as the timekeeper.

6   The other players each have to make up a headline consisting of four words, each word beginning with one of the four letters.

7   Players are not allowed to change the original order of the letters.

8   Players are not allowed to leave out one of the letters or put in additional words.

9   Each player should write down one headline and then say 'finished'.

10 The headlines must be correctly spelt. (Use a dictionary to check words you are unsure of.)

11 Work to a time limit of two minutes. Players completing a headline successfully within the time allowed score one point. The player who is the first to finish scores two points if their headline makes sense.

12 Move on to each player in turn for new letter sequences.

13 Some letter sequences, like 'XXXX', will be impossible. Others like 'ZQYV' will be very difficult. Try and use letters which can be easily made into headlines. For example, 'MDRW' could give the following headlines:

MAD DONKEY RUNS WILD

'MY DAUGHTER'S ROMANTIC WEDDING'

MINERS DISRUPT ROYAL WALKABOUT

MYSTERY DISEASE REACHES WAKEFIELD

MINISTER DONS RED WELLIES

14 The winner is the player who scores most points at the end of the game.

Punctuation and word order

Collect all the headlines you can find containing punctuation marks. Include any printed marks that are not letters, like dots, dashes, asterisks (*), brackets, inverted commas and currency signs. List them in a table with the most frequent ones at the top and the least frequent at the bottom. What do you notice about the order of frequency? What do you notice about full stops in headlines?

Points of view

The real story behind the headline is almost always more complex than the story that is published. Headlines appear to summarise the news but they also put a slant on it. The story of the *Three Billy Goats Gruff*, for example, could be headlined, CLEVER GOATS FOIL MUGGER, but they could also read, BRIDGE SUPERINTENDENT KILLED BY HOOLIGAN GOATS.

Think of a well-known fairy tale, nursery rhyme, novel, film, or play. Write two headlines for it reflecting two different points of view.

Front page

To do this activity, you will need to prepare it in advance.

Keep a notebook handy and in the course of a week find out information to create two news stories. One story should be about your neighbourhood, the other about school. Don't cover events reported in the local press. Find your own 'exclusive' stories.

Write the stories up briefly, complete with a headline for each. Next, work in groups and create the front page of a newspaper using all the stories written by your group. If any two stories deal with the same subject, see if you can trade with another group, or find a way to combine the news stories. Your group will need to make editorial decisions about which is to be the lead story, and whether the headlines could be improved.

Some headlies!

Sometimes a mistake can lead to an interesting discovery or idea. Mistakes in language often do this. Some pupils collecting news reports of the Gulf War in 1992 arranged a wall display to show how different papers gave the news a different slant. When they put a banner heading across the top it read 'Gulf War Headlies'.

Someone had accidentally omitted the letter 'n' of 'Headlines'! The creation of the word 'headlies' was a happy accident which they decided to keep. It doesn't exist as a dictionary word and it is not likely to catch on, but it nevertheless has a meaning. Write a definition of what you think it means.

Suppose it means 'headlines that don't tell the truth', or 'headlines that are difficult to believe'. Write some headlines of your own that would take some believing. Here are some examples:

ANGRY PUPILS DEMAND MORE HOMEWORK

GOVERNMENT ABOLISHES TAXES

SCHOOL LEAVING AGE RAISED TO 21

NORTHFIELDS COUNTY HIGH WINS FA CUP

ALL PARTIES AGREE ON EDUCATION POLICY

MARTIANS HAVE LANDED

WOMEN OUTNUMBER MEN IN CABINET

Ambiguity

Here are some examples of **ambiguity**, or double meaning, in headlines:

GENERAL FLIES BACK TO FRONT

PM WINS VOTE OF CONFIDENCE BUT MORE LIES AHEAD

LOCAL GIRL DOES WELL AT DOG SHOWS

POLICE FINALLY GETTING SHOT AT PROMOTION EXAMS

WOMAN SAYS CORPSE IN GARDEN A PLANT

Ambiguity happens all the time in everyday uses of language but we usually understand what is really meant and ignore, or are amused by, the alternative meaning. Subeditors keep an eye open for ambiguities because if they get into print the paper could look ridiculous.

The danger of ambiguity in headlines is higher than in ordinary language because a good headline has to be short. Write a dictionary definition of 'ambiguity'. Check it against one or two dictionary versions. If you like, you could try to write an ambiguous headline of your own.

Good news, read all about it

In this activity you are going to write a news story about a friend or relative. It can be anything you like but it must be true. Go for something cheerful. Aim for about a hundred words. You can also write your own headline and put your name to the story.

Make the story really interesting and entertaining through your style of writing. Don't be afraid to exaggerate (within reason!). There is nothing particularly special, for example, in the news about Alan Dale (see Text A). It is only the fact that he is a TV celebrity that makes him newsworthy, but the article seems interesting because of its descriptive language and punchy, short paragraphs.

Here are some imaginary headlines for stories that could well be true but which have never been told:

GRANNY'S BICYCLE DASH TO BETTING SHOP

FOUR-YEAR-OLD BITES CAT

BIRTHDAY TREAT FOR BIGGEST BUDGIE IN LIVERPOOL

'MUM'S A COMPUTER EXPERT'

DYNAMIC DUO COLLECT SILVER PAPER MOUNTAIN FOR GUIDE DOGS

SARAH DANCES HER WAY TO GOLD MEDAL

SUPERDAD SCORES HIGHEST INNINGS EVER

News like this celebrates everyday life, making it special and out of the ordinary.